Leaving
the
Nest

Dorothy Baird

TWO RAVENS
PRESS

Published by Two Ravens Press Ltd
Green Willow Croft
Rhiroy
Lochbroom
Ullapool
Ross-shire IV23 2SF

www.tworavenspress.com

ISBN: 978-1-906120-06-1

British Library Cataloguing in Publication Data. A CIP record for this book can be obtained from the British Library.

Designed and typeset in Sabon by Two Ravens Press.
Cover design by David Knowles and Sharon Blackie.

Printed on Forest Stewardship Council-accredited paper by Biddles Ltd., King's Lynn, Norfolk.

The publisher gratefully acknowledges subsidy from the Scottish Arts Council towards the publication of this volume.

Scottish
Arts Council

About the Author

Dorothy Baird was born in Edinburgh. After travelling widely, including a year spent teaching English in France and the Soviet Union, and two years in the West Midlands, she returned to the city in 1989 to bring up her three children. For many years she was a tutor of English and Communication Skills for adults with learning disabilities. She now facilitates creative writing groups for adults in mental health centres and in the community, and leads writing workshops for children. She also runs a correspondence course in creative and therapeutic writing, and is a Human Givens therapist.

Acknowledgements

Some of these poems have been published in magazines:

Acumen *(Joe, Without Edges, Letting Go, Badger Watch, Call of the Night Child)*, Aireings *(Curves)*, Cutting Teeth *(Nursery Blues, Autumn)*, Decanto *(Failure)*, Distaff *(Yin and Yang, Street Fear)*, First Time *(You Could Say it Was an Honour)*, Genie in the Bottle *(Bella Donna)*, Giant Steps *(Re-think)*, New Writing Scotland *(Dawn at Benares)*, Orbis *(Harvest Moon, Pregnant Pause, Christening)*, Penine Ink *(Wearing the Burka)*, Poetry Scotland *(By Design)*, Resurgence *(Akin)*, Smoke *(Revisiting No. 33)*, Spokes *(Making Bread, Jessica)*. *Letting Go* was a Diamond Twig Internet Poem of the Month.

Poems published in anthologies include:

The Birth – Into the Gold of Flesh (Women's Press). *Joe, Pregnant Pause, Christening, Without Edges* – With My Heart in My Mouth (Rudolf Steiner Press). *Christening, The Sick Child, Relief, Nursery Blues, Letting Go, Recipe for a Mother, Pregnant Pause, Revisiting No. 33* – The Winding Road (Hawthorn Press). *Wearing the Burka* – Cool for Qat by Peter Mortimer (Headline Press). *Growing Up* – Images of Women (Arrowhead Press). *Demeter,* here renamed *Missing* – My Mother Threw Knives (2nd Light Publication).

Introduction

My children have not left the nest yet. But each day, though not conscious of it, they are becoming more and more ready to do so, in a process that really began the day they were born. This process for me as mother has been, and continues to be, filled with moments of intense joy and loss – often, paradoxically, experienced at the same time. Many of the poems in this collection have arisen out of those small yet striking moments of mothering when I have stopped and wondered, felt fear, or given thanks.

But life isn't just about being a mother (though it might feel like it at times) – and the whole of life is filled with such fleeting, significant moments. Writing about those that have occurred, whether in Wester Ross, India, Moscow or Edinburgh, is my way of exploring the meaning in my experiences and those of the people around me. It's about trying to do the impossible: to fully honour the essence of a moment. As if, in writing, I can hold the butterfly long enough to see it truly, before I let it go.

I hope you enjoy the poems.

Dorothy Baird
Edinburgh 2007

For Paul Matthews
who set me on my way

Contents

Revisiting No. 33

Her home was up a clutter of stairs,
a twist of darkness, where the tap tap
of her stick tipped your spine.
Black skirts. Black shawl.
Fingers like heather roots.

The wind lists now at the glass,
unpicks the paint, scatters cherry blossom
from the trees folk used to say
should have been rowans,
and there's nothing there to show
the shiver of air
that hung around her door
– those clenched-heart dares
to ring her bell and run away.

It was said she never ate, it was said
she ate the dust, it was said
she smothered children,
it was said she knew the small talk
of the moon – so many words
chased us along the street
till we'd hurtle in a heap
behind a hedge
and believe
and not believe each other.

School Lesson

What was physics but bulbs
and batteries and lights that died
like the refusal of an answer,
and bulls' eyes from the butcher's
carved bloodily from corpses
on a hook and passed in class
over words we couldn't see
without a rising gorge, and that day
Sheila spilt acid on my tights
and we learned first-hand
how black nylon pings
into holes, and the Headmistress
hurried me out, bare-legged,
to buy a new pair lest anyone
ask too many questions.

First Period

No cymbals, no cheers, no
cabbalistic celebrations
at this beginning. Just
my secret blood
and the smooth cold of the toilet

as somewhere, perhaps,
an unborn child,
claiming the source of this blood
for its own,
smiles
at the thought of resurgence;

while my childhood
shimmers like a loch
in whose clear water
I can no longer dive.

Four Years Old

The strong arm of the wind
flexes the trees. They sway,
shifting darkness into patterns
of light, shaping air
into blue segments. The girl next door
bellows *My Bonnie*
Lies Over the Ocean as she flies
on the swing at the hub
of her happiness, the minor key
an expression only of the wind
turning her heart like a prayer wheel.

Badger Watch

It wasn't so much the badgers
I'll remember, though their shadowy
forms caught my breath
as they rustled in the earth mounds

and nosed in twigs and bluebells – no,
it was rather the waiting,
the five of us, faithful
to the silence we'd agreed on,

crouched downwind, while night
eased itself among the trees
and sheep coughed in distant fields,
when we learned the language

of each other's face; how
in the sweeping dark
we dwindle to a beating heart,
and how in the long emptiness
the sliver of hope still rises.

Dogs in Agra

They roam at night, rangy, uncollared,
a tyranny of yobs, bone taut,
determined. One hour ... two ... I lie
in the throes of imagined fear,
the door frail against their wild eyes
and slavering gobs, till the noise
impales itself on exhaustion
and impending light.

The woman behind the desk wobbles her head:
You must be forgetting them, she says: *it is
only dogs.*

We trade our string beds for a garden home
with thick walls and a holy man
who wakes us with his chanting
and the soft rainfall of his silver bell.
We forget about the dogs.

Except sometimes, as pink dawn
slides its lover's hand across the Taj, we
stumble over one, stiffening
in the stench of a gutter – and once,
by the river, where bodies
become ash, become air,
we see one half-floating
in marigold-strewn water.

Dawn at Benares

Darkness. A drumming of women
slapping and whacking
dirt from clothes. Knee-deep
in the Ganges, suds floating
on the black water like flowers.
There is no sign. No movement
of the earth that asks for change

but change is written on the river
and somehow the almost-light
floats in: that grey-blue time we give
no name as if we favour the gloaming dusk,
the twilight, the crepuscule,
when all promises are rescinded
and we are comfortable in regret

and not this eastern moment
when the sun begins to rise
over the smudged line above the scrub
in its veils of gauze
and we fall away
like smoke, like water, like thought
into this slow power of movement.

Train to Pyatigorsk (Ukraine)

Three days and nights. A moving house.
In this tiny room I share snores and gherkins
with a babushka and her daughter
and a man in a suit who reads a fat book
with a bookmark of Lenin.

Beyond the window is an emptiness,
a beautiful despair
where only silver birch trees
dare to stand upright
in the wide sweep of horizon.
Out there is a madness
gathering at the glass
pressing its cold nose like a beast.

In here we sip amber tea
to the rhythm of the wheels,
nod across the miles.

Moscow Banya (steam baths)

Large women lounge
as if the air were silk, breasts
dolorous as Sundays, bellies
soft as rising dough,
the small triangle of hair
a uniform amongst the complexity
of flesh; their script of veins,
birthmarks, stretchmarks, scars,
puffed ankles, bruised thighs, a drama
of queues and cold relieved
at the doors. Here only the young
have uncreased limbs and babushkas
uncouple the iron they're made of
when they shed their clothes.

The Homecoming

The whole world has shrunk to this house
beside the river and the hill.
And I am glad
to watch the moon rise
between the ash tree and the rowan
and see the subtle changes in the leaves
whose language is as strange
as any foreign tongue.

Street Fear

Footsteps behind
are heavier than mine
uptempo drumming
with fear. Don't
worry. It's
your night
too – your right
to walk alone. Just
hurry...
    The hoary night
closes
dark fingers
round me. Animal
bursts
into possession – beyond
its civilised cage;
these feet,
    this fear,
        this certainty
of headlines horror
gloats upon... Don't
hurry. Just
worry...
    My neck
crawls
as if his fingers
please themselves already. Nearly
home. My haven. His footsteps
heart beat behind me. I stuff a scream
down my throat, slice up
the steps, legs woolly
over the sanctum.

Breathtight
at the window, my torch eyes beam
a shadow. Is he strolling
his sleep on –
            or is it him,
his throbbing fading
in the street he stalks,
lion of the night,
his prey
slipped
through his fingers,
down her hole?

Akin

Sister,
    I know your wiles; I've used them myself
to catch the darkness of man's eyes, laid my curves
deliciously around him, laughed
sunlight in his mornings
                and

Sister,
    I sing your songs
in words heard as I walk with you nearby,
                and catch your eye
in the turning of a leaf;
gleam of a glance you dance in

              – so why,
Sister,
hold your secrets to your heart?
Come, speak with me,
              trust in me,
for I would grow more kind.

Harvest Moon

This is the night of the moon. She rises
blushing at what she sees.

She is in our hearts, blank eye,
round pearl, face full

with an ice, not wine: she drinks
no wine to fill her, though she would forget

the night within us, turn her blind eye
beyond the sky. Through the long grass

night dew is creeping. The moon cries
upon this grass. In the morning

I will see her tears. She will be gone,
swooning into the arms of dawn.

Pregnant Pause

Drawn outdoors to smell the waking earth,
I feel you wake
to flit against me, bird
or fish or babe; this spring
you are all three,
and I who sought fulfilment in my words,
wishing for a moment to be God
and give new form a voice,
find now the poetry I strove for
in the blossom and the tulips' fire,
in your fledgeling life within me.

Jessica

Born three weeks,
you are a puckered cry
and eyes that sink into
the lap of wordless sleep;
no dreams can twitch

your lids – unless
of half-remembered days
unreeled before your birth:
in sleep forgetting all
you may have seen

in dark waters waiting
for the signal to be born
– as when at death
the film of all that's been
is flashed before our eyes.

You have come,
changing the world irrevocably,
slight though your touch still is
upon the spider's web
that holds us all.

The Birth

Longer ago than leaps my mind,
I, not I, a younger older wiser me
welled with the world,
a softness, strong in woman, all
feeling full with being, a gown
of dusk-down blurring, holding
healing in my heart, was round womb, wound
with seasons, wise with moon
with whom I shared my tidal seas,
sleeping while her eye was open.

I was the world was me. We rolled in
darkness down together, deep-
drunk with being; until he grew,
a grumble in my depths at first, and grew,
a grit that gathered snow,
ice-cold and calling sounds
that wounded me, until too heavy-
heaped in me he lay; and long I laboured
pressing him, his icy wind,
aloud into the light.

He was my son, this hard and separated form
that left me, seeking light; my night
would smother him, he said, seeing nothing
with my eyes, but sure that his were true.

Alone I live in shadows shoring up his dreams
and wait with all my woman wealth
until his dawn delves in my sea, and thaws
his ice-bound thought. Then soft and hard
will lace with love; his lips of light
will call my name, and all my moon-warmed night
will wave into his word, and heal the hurt
of cloven hearts – the world will hear our gasp
of oneness in our birth.

Christening

We mark this day our wonder
that you have come, teaching us
to be your father and your mother
opening our eyes to your enormous joy.

We remember your birth
when you burst upon us from the crumpled womb
and breathed, calm and still,
as though this was no more than you'd expected,
while we held you as though you'd break.

We name you Thomas, but doubt not
that we love you, nor that your heart,
like the hills, has its own wisdom.

We name you Arthur: be the king
and leader if you will, but be too the farm boy
who smiles when the sun rises.

We name you William, and ask no more
of you, than the flowers, sweet William,
for they become themselves
                              and gladden our hearts.

Thomas Arthur William; our son,
our sun: may we two shine
like the moon, in your light.

B.C. (Before Children)
A.D. (In the Year of Our Lord)

I cannot remember how it was
before you were here – how I must have wakened
in the full light of morning
and followed the whim of the day.

I cannot remember noticing
how precious my thoughts were,
how I could ravel and unravel
their long skeins without breaking

the thread. Nor can I remember
the way futures beckoned
with the open arms
of a forest in full sun. A mist has fallen,

and though the turning point
is part of a long story, it is the real beginning.
Now day breaks in the darkness
with your cry, and I shuffle

the corridors of your palace, bow
before your mush-encrusted throne,
strive to translate
the chuckles and bellows of your reign.

Nursery Blues

I do not know where it is,
the warm smell I reach for
in the night, the warm milk
that keeps the screams away from me.

She's gone. The door took her away.
I hate doors; they are mouths
eating my mother, the yawn
of moon-dark swallowing the sky.

The others play with their toes,
find their thumbs to warm them,
burble in their baskets.
But there's a wail in me,

a giant sound that keeps on coming
and my thumb is too small
to stop its flood, and the shoulder
my cheek lies on and the hands

that smooth my back
do not smell of her,
and even the light,
without her, is black.

The Sick Child

She breathes with mouse breath,
a faint fustiness drifting from her lips.
We sit, watching blue-tits on the nuts,
lulled by the syncopated rise

of lungs. She is a rag doll in my lap,
head under my chin, hands dangling,
empty of the fizz that fires her
into endless moving.

A car passes. The sun strolls
beyond the window. She leans
against me, curving to fit
my hollows and I would grow

another skin to wrap her in
my darkness
till she's ready again
to push towards the light.

Making Bread

Images mock me of earth mothers
mixing their staff of love
with skilled fingers.

I wrestle in a snowstorm;
defiant lumps lie sullen in a cracking mass
or cling like porridge to my hands.

A long time I have pummelled my soul
– till it can stand alone;
but thorns grow harsh without their rose...

Hey, you women at my elbows,
stop laughing and weeping;
I'm trying to unfold my petals,

but the frost of the years is upon me.

Leaving the Nest

1.

One by one they crawl, heave,
scrabble their small bodies
and too-long legs
from the cramped dark
onto the sloping roof where,
primed by some unseen force,
their wings – those limp wet-washing wings –
remember the old story
and know the rush of air and flex
of bone will hold them
– so they leap, one by one,
into that windy stuff,
into the new darkness
of the holly tree and the touch
of swaying bark between their feet.

2.

Today my baby sets off
down the road on her bike
for the first time alone,
wobbling and waving wildly.
I watch the bend take her away,
breathless with a pang
of prayer that conjures light
around her like a shield of air. Oh,
she isn't going far – just
round the corner to see a friend
but the cord they never cut at birth
tightens across a vast topography
of canyons, torrents and
dangerously shifting earth.

Relief

A blue afternoon in August.
They slip from a familiar shape
to a space where all that is
is their absence.

Black-headed gulls squawk
over a yoghurt carton.
A woman whose grey hair is long
as an old mermaid leans
into the shelter
of her man's thick jumper.
Water laps against the jetty.

I imagine their paddles
turning like windmills, the boat
bumping against waves, water
the colour of a bruise, lifted into light
that trails down arms. Her eyes
will be furrowed with determination.

She is only eight.

The bench hardens. A wind picks up.
The woman's hair wafts like seaweed
against the shoulder of a rock.
My watch is barely moving. But
I'm well-behaved, sip cups of tea, until
the sea has swallowed them
and the afternoon's
turned black.

And then the headland
gifts them back, paddles
scything the air. 'Seals'
she sings, 'Out there,
so close we heard them breathe!'

The mermaid smiles
as if she understands.
I press my palms,
smooth out the nail marks
buried in my hands.

Failure

I want to believe my arms can catch you
as you stumble on the steps,
or comfort you
when you trap your finger in the door,
or wake in the night
with wide and frightened eyes.

I want to keep the light
of your fool's wisdom.

But you trawl relentlessly
for the missing pieces in your world,
scrape with the knife of your eleven years
at the skin of my attempts,
and ask again and again
but why?
                And now
your eyes are the scales of justice
in an unbalanced world
– and answers flit
away from me, too slippery
too sad
to be caught.

Breaking the News

We thought we weren't ones for pets.
How much his soft black back
has twitched into our hearts this news
lays bare: we weep. Even you,

whose eyes know years of drought,
are moved tonight
with what seems a double end.
Who would be a parent now?

It can't be done. For years I've shielded
against blistering sun, wrapped
against cold, cradled against hurt.

It must be done. Wrapping my dressing-gown tight
I cross the landing.
Her room has never seemed so far away.

Missing

The syllables of your name catch me off-guard
– I hear them everywhere as I hear you
calling me, calling me
in the fields, in the silence
where prayer falters, in the pulse
of my heart that betrays me
with its insistent beat.
I am wordless. Only the harsh sound
of my womb calls and calls again,
like a curlew at the end of longing.

Night Walk

In his bag a warm drink and a torch
he wasn't asked to bring.
The weight of the cold phone
in my hand is a measure
of the distance between us... *Aw, Mum*
I won't need that
                as he eases himself
into the thicket of boys, while I stand
and watch them diminished
by the hills and the night.
Ocht they'll be fine out there
in the sweep of the stars and the rocks
and all the empty dark.

– Won't they?

Rugby

You snatch the ball. Dummy
dodge. Wham into a wall
that wears a shirt. Fall. Run on.
Nothing exists beyond the pitch,
the shifting shapes of the teams,
the pattern you belong in.

Your feet are size eleven.

I cannot believe you ever lay
in the tilting dark
of my womb. I cannot believe your fingers
curled like flower tendrils round mine,
your eyes angled upwards
as the markings on a pansy's face
turn towards the sun.

Now, when you lumber off the pitch,
tribal man within your tribe,
the distance is careful between us.
When you smile our eyes are level.
Soon I will be looking up to you.
In the car home I am cold with watching.

You are sharp with sweat
and have an answer for everything.

Defiance

It rained on her tenth birthday.
It rained on the trampoline
she had begged for a year
to be given. She watched
it gush from the sky,
her pale face set
against the gods.

Finally she gave up,
removed her socks and
padded down the path
to bounce and bounce
among the stotting rain
waving her umbrella
like a trophy.

Letting Go

Up the mountain path this afternoon
in the midst of pines and Douglas firs,
new shoes rubbing on my toes,
boys in long shorts shriek
from the bridge and rise
with a triumphant toss of wet hair,
to shake the last traces of disbelief
that they've done it
from their angular souls.

How the trees bear witness:
how they watch our small courageous lives
and simply let them go,
living for the next breath of wind
to lift their needles
and stroke their pitted skin.

Growing Up

My daughter poses in front of the mirror
with nothing on. She leans, arms stretched
above her head, trying on faces, and I wake
from months of blindness: this preening girl
has wintered in the darkness of her clothes
the curve of hips, the swell of breasts.
She's pouting now, lips in league
with her sultry gaze. She sways, provocative
as a lap-dancer, her feet just missing
the plastic figures she was playing with
half an hour before.

Mothers

We are potters who never rest,
shaping our children, fashioning
uniqueness with our busy hearts,

and we are the light
that seeps into curtains and floorboards,
shifting their molecules into a home,

our whole body strung
to the tune of concern, an ear on edge,
gauging the register of silence.

We orchestrate the days,
balancing harmonies of the insignificant,
remembering the forgotten.

Each morning we rise,
arms already stretched
to span our children's griefs,

and hoard moments like gold,
so we may feel the weight
and glister of their past.

Bella Donna

I am lady of crumbling walls and grasses
where eyes no longer pry
and no laughter leaps upon the air.
Beauty is mine
and name of beauty,
but my bells are all but silent:
they toll one sound
in midnight's passing hour
for love that dies and
dies. No lover lies
within my arms, has ever lain
but one kiss cast death
upon his lips.
I gather night into my shade
fold it into fruits
of grief, and gently smile
my dark smile.

Wearing the Burka

How hard her eyes work
without the slant
of cheekbones catching the light,
the many gestures of her mouth.
Her world is visor-shaped, as she
pushes her buggy by the park, or
mumbles in shops a mouthful
of cloth – it flaps a semaphore
of syllables against her lips.
Her small son watches
the grey curtain
that contains his mother, learning
about eyes and hands and ankles: how
surprising they are, like young twigs
stripped of their bark.

The Gardener

Each year winds blow more fiercely
through the coral of her bones
and the ground grows further
from her stiffening back, but still she
kindles cyclamen, begonias, geraniums,

tucks cuttings into terracotta pots,
whispers like a horse tamer
and the sap hears her and obeys.
When she dies she says we must mulch
her round her favourite azalea

fork her into the camellia bed,
so she can rise in their green stems,
filter into petals that open pinkly
in the sun, be held finally and briefly
in the wide arms of air.

An Unruly Gratitude

How can I write about this mothering time
when every dawn finds waiting for me
a huge stone to heave
of dirty clothes, open mouths,
sticky floors, the soft and urgent need
for more than I can give

– when all the weary repetitions
I swore would not be mine
still slip from my lips,
when I use all ruses
to stall for time
so my mind can taste
the luxury of an uninterrupted thought?

                    How
can all this be recorded –
when in the moment of pause,
such as this one, *now,* my words
rear treacherously towards
the brazen wonder I learn
again and again from their eyes,
towards the sense of story
these children bring
to my unravelled days?

Oh Buddha, you would understand
my unruly gratitude,
would honour the sunlight
for the way it plays
within the shadows
of the beech tree.

Filling the Well

Sometimes the day comes
when you have given everything
in your attempts to be everything
to everyone. You will know this day
when your small bird cannot flex
its wings against the wind,
when your sun cannot heave itself
over the horizon, when you lower
your bucket into the well and hear it
thud against the clay.

When this day comes you must take off
the smile that is no longer truly yours,
and batten down your heart
that now betrays you with its giving.
You must hold your hands
about your ears, for their voices
are the siren calls that will bind you
to them. And you must walk or limp or run
through the door you can barely see
into the darkness of a lonely room,
into the ocean of an empty moor,
into the wide arms of the forest,

and sit or walk until from deep within
a trembling starts to pulse,
and your diviner's hands sense
what the oak tree and the sycamore
and the worm that flicks its tail
as it bellies into the earth
all know: the source
is the same source
you are thirsting for. Drink deeply.
Be still. Be slow. The world can find its way

without you. For you must drink
until your well is filled, until your feathers
plump, until a new sun rises
in the winter of your eyes. Then,
and only then, may you return,
and when they see you, lush
against the light, let them
stand back a little further than before
and be amazed...

By Design

The sky holds me
and the heather holds me
and the line of my head
to my feet is suddenly strong

like the masterly stroke of an artist
bringing vertical to the picture's lines
and even the rock with its lichen stain
and the pippit on the fence post seem

somehow deliberate as if chance
had its own design – and I think of all
the fields of light
raying towards me, shaping

me, and how my movements also
shape the light, shifting it
to make a space for me, how
the pippit and the black-faced sheep,

the fence post and the heather all
press themselves
into this receiving air, and how
this intricate relationship feels

like a kind of love, like
ordained patterns in a courtly dance
where unspoken questions
meet their answers in another's glance.

Victims of War

I

The Old Soldier

Out with his daughter,
skylarks on yo-yos
of song in clear air,
tractor churning earth,
he sensed the pieces
falling into place,
could touch the fragile links
that bind the past together,

but when mud clogged
and squelched and spattered
and leaf smoke wreathed
his damaged lungs, he longed
to blind the inner eye
that reeled from shards of memory,

and drank

till the beast usurped his limbs,
and his fist, fired with rage,
lashed out at the innocence
on his wife's defeated face.

II

Untangling the Past

I choose the hymns,
wonder what flowers
you might like,
unable to grasp
this sudden lack of you
beside the fire.

Memories are stones now,
knots I can't untie.
You will never know
I might forgive you, one day,
for the aching hallway
where I heard you,
like a tortured bull goaded
by the sting of whisky
in your wounds, bellow
as your hand ricocheted
off mother's whitespun face.

None of us were talkers.
Silence feigned its balm
on a pain that calcified
in the past's dark lochans.

But now you're dead, the wind
blows your presence on the hills
less tangled than in life,

though I will not hear you laugh
like you did in the fields,
when I bounced beside you
on the shiny leather,
watching your thick hands
thread the steering wheel
as we channelled brown earth
in our wake.

III

The Wife's Mosaic

I'm not silly: I know
when doors clacked behind me
gossip swarmed like midges
in the gloaming; that folk
scrolled my face for signs

they'd hoard all day
to lighten the tedium
of their winter's tea.
But I held my head up,
said nothing: after all,
I'd married well, they said –
the big house, all that land
were mine, and vows
in those days were vows.

So I put panstick on the bruises,
tucked the pain away
like a hideous wedding gift
you can't throw out –
I'm only telling you now
because he's dead
and I need to carve away
the burden I've carried
so long it's like a growth.
But the mosaic of memory
has gold within its fragments
too – and I mind father and daughter
would come from the fields
complicit as lovers, the wind's wide blow
in their clothes and laugh
light into our tea.

Nor did she ever know
the power of mud and rain
to salt his unhealed wounds,
nor knew the drink he used
to weld his shattered heart
betrayed him,
and for these gleams
I'm glad.

Have I forgiven him?
What does it feel like
to forgive? He's dead now,
and that's an end to it.
I shall remember
summer evenings
when he teased me
from the ironing,
his smile, wide as the glen
he'd come from,
his broad shoulders
and his Sunday hands
beside mine at the front
of the church, his voice
like rich gravel
leading the hymns,
underlying their song.

Medicine

Three gulls on the fence
fold their wings,
look on with sharp eyes
and restless heads.

It is all I have,
these images. I write them
like a prescription. *Get well
get well*, the sea whispers
from its rumpled grey.
What are prayers but the iron
of words we forge
to rein in our wildest fears? Death,
that's what I'm talking about.
That no longer, never again-ness
we don't believe in, until
we have no choice.

The gulls have gone now
lifting their bodies
into the holding air,
leaving their image
like the pale slip of sweetness
on a spoon.

The Power of Words

They say harsh words can harm a plant;
a discordant music, an intention
underlayed in sound distorts
the molecules in sap. It wilts,
grows crooked, closes its cells
to goodness in the earth. We
are made of water too. Speak gently
to me. I would like to bloom.

Foot and Mouth

We leaned on the farmer's fence,
watched his eyes cloud
as he spoke, while the children
poked plump fingers through the wire
straining for a stroke of lamb.

That Easter our car wiped its wheels
on a mat and in a mockery of
Maundy Thursday we washed
our feet in pungent tanks.

Paths across fields were heavy
with blossom, hawthorn berries,
shoots of nettles. Forbidden
to walk them, we paced instead
the promenade, putting greens,
the safe sand by the pier
while in the distance
the column of smoke rose.

The Fairy Lochs – Wester Ross

A plane carrying American soldiers on their way home at
the end of the Second World War crashed here. Everyone
on board was killed.

Two adults three children
trudge into hills
through juniper, heather, the clutch
and grasp of mud.

Bog cotton flickers like will-o'-the-wisps
and the fairy lochs watch us
with their soft eyes
where lilies are white prayers
hovering on the threshold
of two worlds.

We see it then: crumpled scraps
scattered on the slopes
like litter from death's pocket.

A propeller points to the sky
with names we read in silence:
a gravestone

where the dark water stirs
like settling memories
in the smirring rain.

Autumn

It's the dying season,
though *dyeing* is more fitting
for the golds and yellows and browns
that soak into the leaves

and wash the hills
and the lochside with
a maelstrom of reds,
and when the sun shines

no stained-glass window
ever glowed
like the copper beech
at the bottom of our garden: so

this death is
not a simple thing
– and whether or not
you have ever stopped to ask,

the darkness of the earth
still holds in its closed mouth
the old washerwoman's secrets
of a green spring.

Winter

No-one can ever tell
what lies in the white arms
of the snow: the thin curl
of a mouse's ribs, a stag's
last stumbles by the shores
of the loch, a trinket
from a child's bracelet – who knows
what the snow lands on
as it falls like owl's feathers,
like swan down, out
of a grey and silent sky?

Re-think

Beech trees are bare now,
silhouette the sky,
unashamed
of bumps and twists
and tangled limbs.

In baggy jumper
scarf, big jacket
hat, gloves, boots I brave
the biting wind,
mull over morning fears
of growing old.

6th January (Epiphany)

There's a way you can throw a stone
on the frozen loch
that sends it ping ping pinging
into the horizon,
where hills stoop to wonder
at their vanished reflections
and a lollop of dog
veers across the ice
on surprised paws

until cries collar it into stiff grass
snuffling at smells
the air holds like gifts.
There's a way too
to dance upon the ice
that brings the lonely child
into her own futures again

even as the sun gathers its skirts
to sink behind the trees.
Do you know this coming
together of all things
in an open place?
Are you too a bearer
of these riches? Or are you
still journeying, your eyes fixed
on the bright loneliness
of a star?

March

I listen for the creak of spring, for ice
  surrendering to the loch's familiar wet,
    for the small pulse that beats in the snowdrop

 as it opens above the brown earth, shy as a child's smile
 on seeing his sister for the first time.
   The rowan tree is thinking of new stories,

hearing them in the bluster of the wind,
  remembering the witch woman, remembering
    the eye of the pond that looks in two directions at once

as we all do, while the rose thinks about the air
 it will flower into and the fern in darkness
   stretches its fist to knuckle the brown earth.

Persephone

Nothing prepared me
for not seeing around me
what has always been: with
no rustle of evening wheat, no
lapwings tumbling in the morning,
no rough-silk seawater sheathing my shin,
I was less than I had always been
or thought I was.

In time – though its passing
was a strange affair, unmarked
by the crescendo diminuendo
of the sun – I found a certain solace:
darkness is made of many colours
and my eyes grew skilled
as a wine-taster's tongue
in sifting the nuances of shade.

One moon-time for every seed
is a hard bargain. I could have swallowed
a lifetime of darkness
easily, and in my thirst
for the earth's fruit have brought an end
to all fruiting: it seems a mother's loss
is like another night, and this love
that is born when we are
can blight a thousand harvests,
can stay winter from its cusp of spring.

Without Edges

Sometimes when darkness falls
and edges soften into gloaming
I feel you push my pen
and coax the words you wish for
onto paper; I would touch you,
know you –
but my hand stays;
so barely there, you need me to be still
– and listen,
and I'm not good at listening.
But I'm learning.
One day we will laugh together.
One day without edges we will
walk together in the woods
and all the trees will turn.

Curves

They're out in the hills, walking the city away,
working the rusty bellows of their lungs.
The skyline undulates around them.
A curlew calls. The wind catches the faint cry
of a sheep. They don't talk much.

That night on the plain of her bed, he walks
the dip and rise of her body. 'All day,' he says,
'I've thought of you, those hills
like the swell of your curves,
walking the warm folds of their earth.'

She doesn't speak.
Like a cow that uselessly flicks at flies,
all day she's scythed at
thoughts of her mother
humped beneath the quilt,
hair matted like fleece on a fence;

of how years before,
crashing from swings and walls,
she sheltered in the fold
of her mother's arms,
found peace in the deep valley of her breasts.

You Could Say It Was an Honour

I wear evening around me
even when the sun rises
and I watch the young women
glide through damp dust to the well,
pitchers like round bellies on their heads.

Once my belly was filled.
I carried him, more precious than water.
But that was long ago,
when the quickening linked me
to other women, and dreams
of plump limbs beneath the cypress tree
were not darkened by the shade
of a thunderous sky and crowds
fleeing in confusion.

                    I held him.
Sometimes I feel him even now
across my heart
as he once was in sleep.

You could say it was an honour.
And when the lightness of a breeze
blows through my thoughts,
I can see my place
in the pattern of it all,
but mostly I sit, piercing the distance
where haze shimmers over fields,
or watch the babies tumble in the dust,
wincing when a fall draws blood.

Yin and Yang

Moon-like, we have emptied
into days where listening
we gave ourselves to you
in the silence of the night
that holds our secrets.

We bore you sons; in pain
we hid from you,
as we were always
soft and white,
your Mary

gazing with moon-eyes on your world,
so frail and female. But strong
we were, in the silence
we can hold no longer. We shout
that you may hear the marriage in us,
consummated long ago. And ask
when you will kiss awake
the woman in you,
that we may greet our sisters
in your blood?

Joe

Joe
you died three weeks ago
and I did not.

I need a mystic's eyes to see where I'm afraid to look:
(into the meaning of the silver thread).

Too much alive to face the thought of death,
I have felt that all this living
will not end;
echoes of the river, glimmer of the eyes
that confess our spirit to the world;

but it seems we can believe our threads
are strung beyond the stars, yet still run
frightened from the shadows.
I hear the weir, watch the sun mime
its dumb show of reassurance. Life overwhelms,
but death does too. Joe, you stumbled on the knot
that pushed you into darkness. Do you know the answers
I am grappling for?
Do you still hear the weir?

I cannot write of death,
for words are born of life and light and love.
I love the light
blazing autumn on the hills beyond;
this dying season shouts its beauty
in the honest wisdom of the trees.
Beauty in dying? I dare not speak of this.
Let the water echo in my ears,
erase the silent mouthings of the stars.

Shed Moments

1.

Leaning on the desk I put together,
sun through the window
cars half-heard along the road
birds singing in the cherry tree
space gathers around me.
I pause writing these words
listening for all the futures
that hold themselves unwritten.

2.

May this shed shelter me.
May this place with the creak
of branches on its roof
and its four walls be a space
I grow in, reaching out
from its monastic source
to the source of some greater truth
where I find words
like suprising friends, ready
to hold my hand and lead me on.

3.

Let me be my self in this shed
naked in my heart,
opening like a daisy
in the sun of a long afternoon.

A Quiet Holiday

She learns quickly they've gone,
bundling their noise and grins
into the back seat of the car.

She can go where she likes now,
no plump hands under her belly
bumping her to the floor,

but she stalks the house restlessly,
scratching at doors
to hear an answering noise.

At the tap of the dish on the floor
she races from buddleia shade
or the dip in the children's beds

and weaves between the stranger's legs
waiting for the hand to smooth her fur,
the voice to stoke her warmth,

but the spoon clinks in the sink,
the door clicks, and only the dust
dances for her in the light.

Being Alone

Sometimes it takes staying up late
when the cat stares at you in surprise
to know with a jolt
that you're fully alone,

like the owl gliding above dark fields
or the fox following its map of smells
through a maze of streets, or the
one tall larch tree on the hill

whose needles a light breeze strums –
sometimes it takes the strangeness
of an ordinary night
to make you still

and small, so you wait
for the moon to appear
like a magician
from the parting clouds.

In My Shed

Here I am at peace
safe to uncurl
like the fern
at the bottom of the garden
that astonishes
as it unfurls
its green heart.

Beyond the Garden

At the bottom of the garden
the weir tumbles from slow brown
into a frenzied froth
and flows on, otter-sleek.
A small ripple struggles to return,
cliffs against the push of tide:
always dashed, always renewed.

Listen, they are thinking of war.

Upstairs, my children sleep, splayed
across the pillows, hands upturned
and open, the softness of dreams
shaping their faces into a sharp
focus for my heart.

Listen, they are thinking of war.

A thousand miles away, a mother
watches a snake of water
glide through stony banks. Her children
are also asleep: one on her back
so close she doesn't know where she
stops, where child begins. A beetle
scrabbles past her foot, not pausing
to investigate her dusty toes.

Listen, they are thinking of war.

The Bomber's Mother

I will not think of how he died. His birth
with purple skin and blood-smeared
sheets, the faeces and sweat,
was enough.

And I will not think of the dead
who went with him. His father
wants to tell me about sacrifice
and justice and words

that when I sit in the darkness
slip like shadows from my
understanding, and all that I ask

would be to touch again
those broad shoulders and set
before him my tabbouleh
and watch him eat.

Illegitimate

I believed in words once.
His flowed like silver
from a rich man's purse,
lifted me from the beck and call
of bells that snapped my limbs
to attention, from long corridors
with laden trays, from the wild blows
of the drunken cook.

When I told him of the child, his promises
that had been bellows
to our love, dried
like a drop of water on the fire.

I will never forget the click
of his heels, the silence, the swing
of his coat-tails as he left me on the landing
like a leaf dropped by the wind.

They call me imbecile now,
hurl words from the Bible like
stones. I will not speak.
Perhaps I will never speak again.
And surely if the pain of this birth
is as harsh as the judgement
they heap upon me, I will
unleash such fury as to
burst all riverbanks and shake
all friendless stars
out of the sky.

Rumbling Bridge

I have been thinking about how the river
  slides and rolls between these rocks for ever,
  and how its thick snake

slithers through stone
  on the same journey
  and always new,

winding from some spot
  in far away grass, where
  flies dance not knowing

how this spurt or seep of wet
  will end, and not, I'm sure,
  caring much either,

preferring to stitch the air
  with their crazy pattern
  and be gone. I think

I will always think
  about things. But how
  would it be,

just for once, to dance
  or slide
  into the next moment

and let go of everything
  – except the soft eddy of air,
  the long resistance of stone?

Divorced Children

In the slant of morning sun they look
like him. All of them. Each one
with an inflection of eyebrows, a quirk
of nose, the angle at which cheekbones
lock together that show in their clay

the imprint of his hands. One of them
has his father's anger
too. In a heart alert as a wolf's
for darkness it cannot understand.
His cry rips the night

in our house and I do not know
what to do; it is not my arms
that can console him – I am no
she-bear with a quick paw
around his ear; no wide river

that might lull him with its song; no
earth woman who senses
in the hot spoor of panic
the trail to follow – I can do
nothing but hope for light.

The Moment

I am forty-one.
Old enough now
to bless the moment and ask
for nothing more
than that the wings of the white bird
that alights on the spire
of the small church
will so fold
that she lands daintily,
picks her way over the moss
on the cracked tiles
and darts her dark eyes towards me
before she wheels again
out into the blue.

Another Tongue

A shroud of mist has fallen on the hills.
The trees droop like relatives
bowed with grief.

A day for funerals:
'Dreich, gey dreich.'

How the lilt of the hills would sing
in my mother's voice, her words
rich as the broken soil;

Shall I bury them now
these words that lived with zest
upon another tongue... Another time,

before the stares of strangers
the quaint smiles of friends
made celebrities of unassuming sounds,
imprisoning them in fame.

Museum pieces now, my tongue
sticks on the dust of their misuse,

and I look at my child
who is no *slitterin bairn*
with no *baffies*
and no *wee dug daundering*
efter him doon the road

and am sad
that the link of the cord
is too fine for language,
that the words have become strangers
met with memories
by the side of their grave.

Recipe for a Mother

Take one heart and stretch it
until it can withstand laughter
and tears in vast measures
at the same time.

Add a liberal dollop of patience,
bind with a strong sense of humour
and marinade
for at least eighteen years.

Scatter a fine disregard
for dirty washing, untidy bedrooms
and cutting comments, particularly those
made by teenagers.

Chop up several pounds of personal aims
and set aside for a minimum of twelve years.
Add an extra pair of hands, a blind eye, and a deaf ear
to use as needed – and zest
and spice of your choice.

Arrange in a dish with a good helping
of women friends. Ensure the centre
still holds it shape even if circumstances
threaten to dissolve it.

Put in a warm house. Make sure this
is big enough to allow for
exponentially increasing clutter.

Bake through long afternoons
of playing shops, pushing swings, Monopoly,
girlfriend/boyfriend worries, acne and exams.
Keep baking even at night, weekends and holidays.

Turn out just when things become smoother. If
it sinks, decorate with fresh interests.
Use nostalgia sparingly... It's not done yet,
and there are no accolades for your skill,
but still – remember to sit back
a moment in the sun
and enjoy...

Call of the Night Child

Three times my belly has swelled with child.
Three times my breasts have ripened like lush pears
and tingled for a small mouth
to release them. Three times is enough.

Each month now the red flow I deal with
in cramped bathrooms washes away
those plump unfinished knees, the scent of hay
from another soft head and fists
that fold and unfold like flowers. And still,

I know three times is enough. I know it
with the logic of reason and the frail light
of my remembered self. So why is it, then,

when the wind fans through the trees at night
I hear the faint cry of a child and know
it's the fourth one, with her blue eyes
and wheat sung hair, hovering
outside my window, calling
like a loon across the sea: *Let
me in, let me in...*

November in My Shed

Wind rattles the walls
as if it wants to dance;
in the garden the trees
are willing partners,
learning new moves
shaking their hair down.

I can tell my shed wants to join in.

Bass Rock Trip

He's a birthday boy his wife says
helping him lurch into the boat.
Two daughters follow, a son
in dreadlocks. His hands lie
like shells clamped on his lap.
His eyes are wary; time, place –

this day is uncertain, here
in the harbour with the diesel
puffing blackness in his lungs
and the rest of us, strangers,
beside him on benches. We watch
gannets squabble on the rock,

wielding beaks like machetes, or
skim the sea like fighter planes
with black-tipped wings. A daughter
points to puffins as they belly
into water and whirr above the grey,
like toys on wound-up wings. He smiles

at the clouds. His left hand opens
a moment then closes. On the way back
wind salts our faces. He shuts his eyes.
A photo is taken. They will remember
this day. The puffins. Guillemots. Gannets.
His dazed presence. His hands.

The Shape of a Mother

The shape of a mother
shifts in all the years she learns in,
testing the sharpness of her heart
against tomorrow when her children leave.

She hides the truth in her bones.

On wintry days they ache
when she sees in her mind's eye
her home empty as the blue tit's nest
she found, its neat circle of hair,

twigs and a pink scrap of paper
from who knows where, cold
now. But what can she do

but go on doing the small things
she's so good at, lining her nest
with pieces of days, moving her joints,
remembering summer?

Mid-forties

More than a month
falls between my flow
and I know no more
the touch of the moon
in my rhythms.

I am leaving her certainties
her heaving sea no longer
ebbs in my blood
and I mourn
the force that filled me

with the small curl of child,
the shell of three lives
embedded in my sea
whose tides listened
to her soft song.

Kedgeree

The old man has dressed up for lunch:
tweed jacket, striped tie, a careful umbrella.
He orders kedgeree. The girl in the hipsters
and the stripe of bare flesh lays it on the plums
and apples of the plastic cloth
with the finesse of silver service. *'Enjoy
your meal.'* The lightness of Australia

lifts her voice, but he can't hear, so she
shouts, wrapping other customers
with her bellowed warmth: the fugue
of confided truths and gossip halts
as folk glance across, but he just scrapes
his chair and picks up a trembling fork.

Kedgeree. The taste of India.

The screech of rickshaws, the rattle
of trains, arguments, barter; his wife too,
her letters damp with heat, the way
her vowels filled his ears as he read them
under the huge sky and lengthening shadows
of the banyan tree.

He clears his plate, aligns his knife and fork
like soldiers, tucks his umbrella
under his arm. Rising, his chair scrapes again.
He shakes his head as if to beat off flies,
then shuffles out
into the soft and silent rain.

December in My Shed

It is cold in my shed. I have bought
a heater whose halogen glow
is a memory of summer, but its warmth
cannot dispel the damp

that lies on the chair legs
like a shadow of the air. This paper
is softer than it should be too, gentle
with moisture as if it has absorbed

the air's grief, and the walls
that were white and calm are stained
with the residue of rain: a birthmark
edged with brown, the shape

of India, a map for thoughts
to wander through and find,
despite this watery room, a way
into the dusty distance.

A Strange Passing

Sixteen years ago I became
your mother one night
when the moon was full
as my belly and the stars
were midwives to this
strange passing
through which you came
pushed by the rush of water
into light and air
that clothed us both
in shock.

I watch you fill the doorway
now, wearing your man's face
as if it almost fits,

and find myself still rising
gently stunned
to greet you.

Changing Parts

Blood has come to my last child,
my baby, who still sits on my lap
after a bath while I dry her toes.

It pushes me, too, towards
my final fertile years; clots,
floods presage the end of
possibilities I do not wish for
now, but know still their passing
as a nub of loss, as I move
towards the third stage
on which to play my life. The Crone.

I do not know the part.
Who will tell me my lines?

I'm not going to learn any lines!
Surely a crone can improvise,
can speak from the heart, that wise script,
face bare as honesty and heedless
of audience, let others simply
do their best to follow?

Friend

There is no-one I would rather
travel with. When I crouch
in long grass to sense direction
in the wind, your feet share
the pull of my north, your hands
gather light like flowers
at dawn and the sparks from our laughter
ignite the dampest wood.

Poetry from Two Ravens Press

Castings
Mandy Haggith

A new collection of poems by Mandy Haggith, whose writing reflects her love for the land and her concern for the environment - not just in the North-West Highlands where she now lives on a woodland croft, but also in her travels around the world.

'*The poetry here shows real clarity of eye marking the dialogues of nature in a place, be that place the lonely Scottish crofting area that is home, or the course of the River Kelvin through the Lowlands, or a Russian forest.*' **Tom Leonard**
'*Outstanding originality and quality. Impressive for its sharpness, sympathy and decisiveness...*' **Alan Riach**

£8.99. ISBN 978-1-906120-01-6. Published April 2007.

The Zig Zag Woman
Maggie Sawkins

A first collection of poetry by Maggie Sawkins.

'*Maggie Sawkins draws brilliantly on extended metaphor and the surreal to explore painful relationships, mental illness and problematic situations. She writes both from personal experience and beyond it. Her inventive and highly individual voice is always authentic. The taut writing carries emotional weight and sends that shiver up my spine which tells me I am reading real poetry. This is a very exciting first collection.*' **Myra Schneider**

£8.99. ISBN 978-1-906120-08-5. Published September 2007.

In a Room Darkened
Kevin Williamson

A first poetry collection by the founder, publisher and editor of the renowned underground literary magazine *Rebel Inc,* a publication which helped launch writers such as Irvine Welsh, Alan Warner and John King into the public domain.

£8.99. ISBN 978-1-906120-07-8. Published October 2007.

Fiction from Two Ravens Press

Parties
Tom Lappin

Gordon yearns for a little power; Richard wishes reality could match the romantic ideal of a perfect pop song; Grainne wants life to be a little more like Tolstoy. Beatrice looks on and tries to chronicle the disappointment of a generation measuring the years to the end of the century in parties.

Parties is a black comedy about young people getting older, and learning to be careful what they wish for, lest they end up finding it.

£9.99. ISBN 978-1-906120-11-5. Published October 2007.

Love Letters from my Death-bed
Cynthia Rogerson

There's something very strange going on in Fairfax, California. Joe Johnson is on the hunt for dying people; the Snelling kids fester in a hippie backwater and pretend that they haven't just killed their grandfather; and Morag, multi-bigamist from the Scottish Highlands is diagnosed with terminal cancer by Manuel – who may or may not be a doctor. Cynthia Rogerson's second novel is a funny and life-affirming tale about the courage to love in the face of death.

'Witty, wise and on occasions laugh-aloud funny. A tonic for all those concerned with living more fully while we can.' **Andrew Greig**

£8.99. ISBN 978-1-906120-00-9. Published April 2007.

Prince Rupert's Teardrop
Lisa Glass

The story of a damaged woman's relationship with her mother, a nonagenarian Armenian haunted by the genocide of her people by the Turkish Army early in the twentieth century. When her mother disappears, it is left to this most unreliable and unpredictable of daughters to try to find her, in this moving, lyrical and provocative work.

£9.99. ISBN 978-1-906120-15-3. Published November 2007.

Nightingale
Peter Dorward

On the second of August 1980, at 1pm, a bomb placed under a chair in the second class waiting room of the international railway station in Bologna exploded, resulting in the deaths of eighty-five people. Despite indictments and arrests, no convictions were ever secured...

'Nightingale *is a gripping and intelligent novel; it takes an unsentimental and vivid look at the lives of a small group of Italian terrorists and the naive Scottish musician who finds himself in their midst in Bologna in 1980. Full of authentic detail and texture,* Nightingale *is written with clarity and precision. Peter Dorward tells this tragic story with huge confidence and verve.*'
Kate Pullinger

£9.99. ISBN 978-1-906120-09-2. Published September 2007.

Short Fiction from Two Ravens Press

Highland Views: a collection of stories by David Ross.
£7.99. ISBN 978-1-906120-05-4. Published April 2007.

Riptide: an anthology of new prose and poetry from the Highlands and Islands. Edited by Sharon Blackie & David Knowles.
£8.99. ISBN 978-1-906120-02-3. Published April 2007.

Types of Everlasting Rest: a collection of short stories by Scotsman-Orange Prize winner Clio Gray.
£8.99. ISBN 978-1-906120-04-7. Published July 2007.

For more information on these and other titles, and for extracts and author interviews, see our website.

Titles are available direct from the publisher at
www.tworavenspress.com
or from any good bookshop.